This Notebook Belongs To

_____

_____

9

In the end, I hope that this Notebook will be a beautiful memory in your memory box for future generations.

😊 Happy wishes 😊

My greetings

Lovely Places

Made in the USA
Monee, IL
23 March 2022

93387055R00063